AIRCRAFT of the VIETNAM WAR

A PICTORIAL REVIEW

AIRCRAFT of the VIETNAM WAR

by LOU DRENDEL

A Ren Morgan Book

AERO PUBLISHERS, INC.

Published by Aero Publishers, Inc.
1980
All Rights Reserved
COPYRIGHT A. G. LEONARD MORGAN, 1971

ACKNOWLEDGEMENT

My sincere thanks are due to many individuals and organizations for contributing information and photographs for use in this book. I am particularly grateful to Cmdr. Joseph Marshall and Lt. Col. Harvey Ladd of the Office of the Assistant Secretary of Defense, Brig. Gen. Robin Olds, Commandant of Cadets, USAF Academy, private collectors Paul Stevens and George Letzter, and Len Morgan, whose advice and encouragement brought this effort to fruition.

– *L.D.*

CONTENTS

FOREWORD

by
Brigadier General Robin Olds, USAF

Having been a military pilot for over twenty-seven years, my reaction to Lou Drendel's excellent pictorial review is bound to be not just parochial, but downright emotional. Worse than that, I have been a fighter pilot for all those years and to cap it all, my bias is deepened by having flown in the current war in Southeast Asia. With that out of the way, I announce here and now it is not my intention to offer a calm, dispassionate, and completely objective commentary on this publication. I cannot do that.

Military aircraft, and the men who build, maintain, supply, and fly them have been a major part of my life since birth. As the son of a military pilot I grew with aviation. My first memories are of the sight, sound, and smell of airplanes, of the talk of the men who flew them, and of the aura and impact of that sphere called the wild blue yonder. No wonder I wanted to fly before I could even tie my shoes. And no wonder it never occurred to me in my exuberance and youthful self assurance that I might not qualify. I happily entered West Point with no other thought. And happily, my dreams came true.

The war in Europe and the responsibilities of command at the tender age of twenty-two brought a degree of accelerated maturity and experience that solidified and gave direction to the dreams of youth. The growing sophistication of design, construction, maintenance, and operation of the implements of air power provided challenge and opportunity for the translation of burning ardor to channels of action.

Thus, as I leaf slowly through the pages of Lou Drendel's review of the aircraft of the Vietnam War I do not see just photographs. I see more, much more. I see the human element, the vision and creativity of designers, the sweat and toil of the maintenance people, the passionate application of the aircrews, the dedication and determination of all who loyally serve America and her people, bound together in common inspiration by that sphere of blue. I also see myself and the thousands of men with whom I have flown over the years. I think of those who yet lie in the corroded, twisted remains of a once beautiful machine, high on the slopes of a jungle clad mountain in a remote and savage land. Or of those who lie with dignity, a carved marble stone attesting their sacrifice to those who care. I see the faces of my contemporaries, etched by the years, but still youthful as the ageless dreamer, and the faces of the young pilots, burning with eagerness and impatience, tight with nervous energy, waiting only for the next flight, the next challenge.

Brigadier General Robin Olds

For these men, flying is not a job, it is a love affair. No pilot calls his plane an aircraft, any more than a sailor calls his ship a boat. The names he uses are many, some even profane, but to him and to him alone, they are terms of endearment. He may call it a bird, a beast, a jug, or a gooney. He may call it a bucket of bolts or old shakey. It can be a dog whistle or a tweet, a bamboo bomber or a box car, a trash carrier or a crowd killer, an aluminum overcast or a peashooter. It can be any of these, but watch it friend, only he can call it that. The use of most of these names by any other than the brotherhood can garner you a flattened nose. Pilots and mechanics are like that, even within the brotherhood there are certain taboos. Before this conflict it was downright dangerous to call a Thunderchief a Thud in the bar at Seymour-Johnson: Since then, 105 pilots have wrought such deeds of valor and sacrifice that the name Thud now proudly bears a bright aura of glory.

This custom amongst pilots is not surface evidence of the hidden mores of a mystic cult. As I said, a pilot is a man in love, a man whose emotional ties with a piece of machinery run deep in his soul. His bluff expressions are protective devices meant to hide that tenderness in his heart when talk turns to flying. To understand this flying must be a part of your life and the machine a part of you. You don't climb into an aircraft and sit down. You strap the machine to your bottom, and you and it become one. Hydraulic oil becomes your blood; titanium, steel, and aluminum your bones; electrical currents your nerves; instruments an extension of your senses. Fuel is the food, the engine the power, the control surfaces the muscle. **3**

You are the heart, yours is the will, you provide the reasoning power. You are something more than earthbound man for every fibre of your being is augmented and expanded by the miracle of the machine. You are tied to it physically and you are part of it emotionally. Together you conquer the bonds of earth and in the words of the poet, John Gillespie MacGhee, ". . . join the tumbled mirth of sun split clouds . . . wheel and soar and swing high in the sunlit silence . . . chase the shouting winds along . . . and, while with silent lifting mind, you tread the untrespassed sanctity of space, put out your hand, and touch the face of God."

To some, these feelings may seem utterly inappropriate in relation to military flying and the grim purposes of war. I assure you there exists no such ambivalence. The realities of danger and the tensions of conflict serve but to heighten the bond between man and machine. When you have rushed head long at tree top level into a storm of flak, when the tracers from an enemy's guns flick past your canopy and you and your bird shudder as others strike home; when you twist and turn in mortal combat, out-numbered and far from help; when you strike with savage thunderous power and wheel in white hot anger toward another Foe; when your bird responds to your impossible demands, slamming you into near unconsciousness with crushing centrifugal force, leaping like a cat when you unleash the full energy of forty thousand horses, beating the earth below with one continuous thunderclap as you exceed the speed of sound, hurling lightning bolts of destruction with deadly accuracy, and then quietly, docilely lifts you home, physically battered, emotionally spent, and numb with weariness, then, that bond is as solid and as personal as any relationship you will ever experience. You settle on the home runway with a sense of deep relief. You and your bird have survived another day and tomorrow is a long way off. As you go through the final shut down procedures, each switch stills a part of the pulsing energy that had been an extension of you. The radio fades to stillness, gyros unwind, hydraulic pressures fall, radar images fade, lights flicker and dim and are gone to blankness, and, as the engine clicks down to silence, air pressure from the fuel tanks hisses free, for all the world like a long sigh before sleep. It's a rare pilot who doesn't feel these things as an act of gentle severance, and his final gloved touch at the bottom of the ladder is a secret gesture of parting.

Think in such terms as you view these pictures. Try to capture the man-machine relationship. Imagine the monsoon rains, the rice paddies, the impossibly thick jungle, the soaring green mountains. Think of searing heat, and sweat drenched men, of dark grey clouds or a searing sun in a pale blue sky. Project yourself onto a flight deck, or deep in bowels of a munitions locker where walls of steel enclose air fetid with metallic stench. Do this, and the pictures will take on true meaning.

Knowing what I know, each page of Lou Drendel's book evokes clear impressions. The F-105 is not sitting on the ramp, but is part of a large force, rolling in on the target ahead of me, screaming down through a sky black with flak and laced with the passage of defensive missiles. The F-4 becomes a wildcat, savagely battling a horde of angry MIGs. The face of Major Fred Haeffner is that of a friend who as a visitor from Danang, got his MIG while flying with the 8th Wing at Ubon. The A-1 is an aging lady, respected for her punch and loved for her role so valiantly played in aiding the rescue efforts for a downed crew. The A-37 is a super Tweet with a sting, carrying her ordnance to the very entrance of a Viet Cong bunker. And look at the grand old lady of them all, older than the men who fly her, veteran of three wars, the Gooney Bird. Still there in the thick of it, very unlady like, and pouring a devastating torrent of lead on the enemy below. The B-52 is unseen, but her presence shakes the very mountains with destructive force. The C-130 lands on a dirt strip and hurriedly unloads as mortar shells bracket her. The KC-135 is an angel disguised as a tanker. Her silver glint as she turns for position for post strike refueling is a happy sight for a weary fighter pilot. But the happiest sight of all must surely be Jolly Green, the CH-3 chopper, as she slows to a hover and lowers her sling to a downed airman hanging by his parachute from the top of a 150 foot jungle tree. To me the RF-101 is a camouflaged streak, weaving alone through a hell of flak, pressing onward to a target far to the north to record the results of an earlier strike. Here is the real unsung hero, for the reccy jock is a loner, fighting his battle with an unarmed bird, raw courage sustaining him, none to witness should "failed to return" be his final epitaph. I see the tiny O-1 circling, circling, drawing fire, marking the targets for the fighters, making repeated passes to insure the positive location of friend and foe. The A-4 whistles through the murk to crunch onto the heaving deck of a carrier. The A-6 probes through cloud and rain in the black of night, her crew's intensely concentrating faces eerily green in the reflected glow of a radar scope, the darkness rent by brilliant bursts of flak, as she closes for a run against the steel mill at Thai Nguyen.

It all becomes a pattern, an image of men and machines at war. Emotion, tension, loneliness, death—borne by wings of fabric, wings of steel. The souls and minds of men noble in the savagery of the holocaust, writing pages of valor and courage, their deeds far to outlast the purpose.

I am grateful to Lou for this compilation. It is more than a review. It is a service to those who love aircraft and a tribute to the men who flew them.

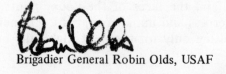

Brigadier General Robin Olds, USAF

A Strange Air War

There has never before in history been an air war like the one in Vietnam. Air superiority, in the conventional sense, is virtually uncontested. And yet, because of complex and sometimes unfathomable political considerations, the job airpower tries to accomplish seems at times impossible, even to its most ardent proponents. This is particularly true of the long and frustrating aerial interdiction campaign waged against North Vietnam. The air war over South Vietnam is not without its frustrations, but for the most part has been fought in a more conventional manner and produced more easily recognizable results. This war, the so-called "in-country" war, produced one of the most stunning military victories in the annals of modern warfare.

Khe Sanh, a sometime Special Forces outpost, sits astride Route 9, the vital link between South Vietnam's coastal cities and her western border. The North Vietnamese attacks on South Vietnamese cities in early 1968 prompted American military planners to view Khe Sanh as an important site. Accordingly, they enlarged its garrison to include 6,000 U.S. Marines and South Vietnamese Rangers, then sat back to await the North Vietnamese reaction. It was not long in coming.

General Vo Nguyen Giap, the conqueror of Dien Bien Phu, personally directed what came to be known as "The Seige of Khe Sanh." Giap poured 40,000 of his troops into the hills surrounding the seemingly vulnerable Marine outpost hoping, it is assumed, to achieve a quick clear-cut victory. An American retreat from Khe Sanh, coming on the heels of the devastating Tet Offensive attacks on South Vietnamese cities, would certainly strengthen the communist bargaining position in any ensuing peace talks. If the Americans chose to stand and fight, they stood a chance of being annihilated by large, human-wave assaults. The thought of what this defeat would do to American resolve on the home front must have seen General Giap beside himself with anticipation. But it was not to be, for Giap had badly underestimated American airpower.

For three months Giap shifted and strengthened his

January 2, 1967: Colonel (now Brig. Gen.) Robin Olds tails a MIG-21 in an action which saw his "Wolfpack" down seven enemy fighters. The son of an Air Corps general, Olds graduated from West Point where he was captain of the football team and All-American tackle. In 1944 he was assigned to the 479th Fighter Group in Europe. By the age of 22 he had flown 107 combat missions, destroyed 24 German planes and had been promoted to Major. After the war he co-founded the first USAF jet aerobatic team. In 1948 he flew Britain's first operational jet fighter and became the first non-Empire officer to command a regular RAF squadron. As commander of the 8th Tactical Fighter Wing based at Ubon, Thailand, Olds was credited with four MIGs and remains the top scorer of the Vietnam War. Brig. Gen. Olds is now Commandant of Cadets at the USAF Academy. *(Painting by the author)*

encircling armies. And for three months they reeled under the heaviest concentrations of conventional airborne ordnance in history. Though communist gunners were able to keep constant pressure on the Marines, never once was the enemy able to launch a major attack on the base. Air Force, Navy and Marine Corps bombers dropped nearly 100,000 tons of bombs on enemy positions during the seige. American transport pilots kept the life line to Khe Sanh open, operating into its 3,500 foot aluminum mat runway. The Marines dubbed the re-supply planes, "Mortar Magnets," for the big transports presented lucrative targets to the communists and almost always drew fire as they unloaded their precious cargoes. But the re-supply effort succeeded and the enemy was kept pinned down by the continous aerial bombardment.

Days became weeks, weeks months and still no attack came from the huge communist force. The few probing attacks launched by the enemy were beaten back in savage fighting. General Giap waited, perhaps hoping for a miracle to present itself, before launching his all-out assault. The weather, always an advantage to the guerillas when at its worst, did not hinder our air operations enough to give Giap the respite he needed to mount a single decisive attack.

Finally, the monsoon began to abate, and with the clearing skies came even more devastating attacks from allied aircraft. Giap would take it no more. He had lost more than a quarter of his force, and the remainder were morally beaten, victims of the unseen B-52s' area bombing and the uncanny accuracy of tactical support fighters. The crafty general who had humiliated the French at Dien Bien Phu withdrew his forces to sanctuaries in Laos and North Vietnam.

In any other war, the stunning defeat handed the enemy would have received enthusiastic accolade. The military leaders who stuck it out at Khe Sanh would have become national heroes. But, since this was the Vietnam War, the big stories to come out of this battle were the insignificant ones: the President's reported insistance that the Joint Chiefs of Staff sign a paper guaranteeing Khe Sanh's invincibility; the American abandonment of Khe Sanh after it had lost its strategic importance. One wonders how historians will view our reactions to this battle. It is certain to be remembered, for it was the first time in history that airpower alone so clearly and effectively denied a superior enemy force his objective.

The air war over North Vietnam has been completely different from the "in-country" war. Begun originally as retribution for attacks by the North Vietnamese on American bases in South Vietnam, the bombing of North Vietnam eventaully became a part of the overall strategy of the war. There has been nothing unusual about the objective of this campaign — the interdiction of war material bound for use in South Vietnam. What has been unusual is the manner in which this campaign has been waged. Against the best military advice available, political leaders decided to wage a gradual and restricted air interdiction campaign. Even within the restrictions set down by Washington, the Air Force has done a creditable job of slowing down the infiltration of South Vietnam. At the height of the bombing campaign it was estimated that North Vietnam was using 600,000 people to repair road damage. During that period, the infiltration of South Vietnam was reduced to five to six thousand enemy soldiers a month. When the bombing was halted the rate rose to 20,000 per month.

Our air superiority over North Vietnam has never been seriously challenged by enemy fighters. Dogfights, in the classic sense have been few and usually end with the enemy's destruction or retreat. The communists have been able to hold their loss rate to a 4 to 1 margin (as compared to almost 10 to 1 in Korea) through the clever use of ground controlled intercept procedures and by avoiding American fighters and going after bomb-laden attack aircraft. The most hazardous aspect of operations over North Vietnam has been the flak. Our restrictive policies have provided Ho Chi Minh and his leaders with convenient sanctuaries, immune from attack by American aircraft. Most of these areas are prime strategic targets, targets which the enemy knew were likely to be attacked eventually. The longer they remained "off-limits," the tougher their defenses became. North Vietnam's communist allies provided radar-directed anti-aircraft ranging in size from 37mm to 100mm. These weapons were brought into North Vietnam through the "off-limits" (to our bombers) port of Haiphong, then shipped overland to the still "safe" industrial complexes of Hanoi. The guns were augmented with Soviet SA-2 Guideline surface-to-air missiles, to form the toughest anti-aircraft defense in history.

But to no avail. The enemy, even with this fantastic array of anti-aircraft weapons, and with adequate time to dig in and train crews, has been unable to stop the destruction of the targets he wanted so desperately to defend. The Air Force, Navy and Marines, through the bravery of their airmen and the technical genius of American avionics experts, have been able to reach and destroy all targets assigned them.

Much has already been said and written about the men who have flown in the air war over Vietnam, often in the face of hazards equal to anything known in World War II. Their courage and dedication to duty in this strange, frustrating, unwanted and unpopular conflict says all that needs be said about the continuing high quality of our armed forces.

This is a book about the aircraft these brave men flew and are flying in Vietnam — the fighters, bombers, attack aircraft and supporting machines provided by American designers and builders. Many of these aircraft are today performing work totally different from that for which they were created, and doing it well, ample proof that "Made in U.S.A." remains a redoubtable mark on any weapon. We may take pride in them, as we do in the men who fly them.

USAF Fighters

February 12, 1966: McDonnell Douglas F-4C *Phantom* mounting camera and Vulcan gun pods streaks toward its target on ground support mission. - *USAF*

Republic F-105D *Thunderchief* with gear and full flaps down returns to its base somewhere in South Vietnam. - *Susuma Tukuna*

Dubbed "The Hanoi Special," this veteran F—105D logged 1500 hours on 450 missions, took a number of pilots through their combat tours and claimed two MIG-17s (note stars beneath canopy). 1st Lt. David B. Waldrop was credited with the kills on Aug. 23, 1967. He flew his 100th mission with 388th Tactical Fighter Wing in this remarkable ship on Dec. 4, the same year. - *USAF*

Lockheed's F-104C *Starfighter* has seen intermittent service in Vietnam, usually in a ground support role. - *Lockheed*

F-105F, seen here at Takhli Air Base, Thailand, grosses out at 54,000 pounds, almost *four times* the weight of Republic's *Thunderbolt* of World War II fame. - *USAF*

The "Arkansas Traveler" flies again. Col. Paul P. Douglas, commander of the 388th Tactical Fighter Wing, points to the insignia on his F-105. Twenty-three years earlier the same badge adorned the P-47 in which he shot down eight German aircraft. *USAF*

Thunderchiefs in action, as visualized in a painting by the author.

A flight of F-105s, led by a North American F-100 *Super Sabre* pathfinder, drops its bomb load on North Vietnamese supply dump hidden in jungle. This photograph taken June 15, 1966, from a McDonnell RF-101 *Voodoo.* - *USAF*

The *Super Sabre* has in Vietnam gained new honors for its builders who made their name in fighters with the P-51 *Mustang* and F-86 *Sabre.* - *USAF*

Two MK-82 high-drag bombs fall away from F-100D making run across Viet Cong base camp in South Vietnam, Mar. 23, 1967. - *USAF*

Trio of *Super Sabres* release a ton and a half of bombs on target near Bien Hoa, April, 1966. - *USAF*

A familiar sight over Vietnam — an F-100 on its way to work. - *USAF*

Brace of Convair F-102 *Delta Daggers* lift from their base in typical scene painted by the author.

Northrop F-5A, as shown here by author Lou Drendel, is called "The Skoshi Tiger" by its pilots. *Skoshi* means "little" in Japanese, and the F-5A is indeed a dwarf as modern fighters go. It weighs slightly more than a *third* as much as an F-4 *Phantom*.

April, 1966; Skoshi Tigers being readied for duty at Bien Hoa. *-USAF*

Boeing KC-135 tanker services F-5A while mates await their turn at the pump. - *USAF*

A forty-seven foot fuselage housing a pilot and 8,000 pounds of afterburning thrust, all supported by twenty-five feet of razor blade wing — that's the F-5A. Imagine the rate-of-roll this combination allows! - *USAF via Geo. Letzter*

The controversial General Dynamics Convair F-111A, the aircraft of radical design, seen here in wings back, high-speed configuration. A spectacular engineering achievement, the type has so far failed to prove itself in its military role. Six were sent into combat and three lost within weeks. - *USAF*

F-4D *Phantom II* equipped with long-range tanks is ready to fly from the United States to its Southeast Asian combat base. - *Paul Stevens*

A pair of 750-pound general purpose bombs are dropped on Viet Cong target by a *Phantom*. - *USAF*

Heavy and ungainly, the *Phantom* looks like anything but a fighter that can hurl itself to 50,000 feet in 110 seconds. But it did just that in a climb-to-height test on Apr. 12, 1961.

Latest fighter to wear the shark's mouth made famous by the Flying Tigers in World War II is this F-4E photographed at Udorn, Thailand. - *Paul Stevens*

Phantoms of the 8th Tactical Fighter Wing's "Wolfpack" enroute to enemy targets. - *USAF*

The latest version of the *Phantom*, the F-4E carries a 20mm Vulcan cannon mounted beneath its nose. - *Paul Stevens*

Victorious Maj. Fred Haeffner paints a red star on the nose of his *Phantom* at Da Nang Air Base, indicating the outcome of his encounter with a North Vietnamese MIG. -*USAF*

USAF Bombers/Attack Aircraft

Cessna's A-37B light attack aircraft began military life as a pilot trainer. Intended for COIN (counter-insurgency) operations, the trim little craft can operate from unimproved strips and carry a wide assortment of machine guns, rockets, flares and bombs.

Via Geo. Letzter

Combat aircraft usually enjoy short lives; by the time a design becomes operational, a better plane has already been test flown. Usually, that is. Here is a remarkable exception to the rule, Douglas' A-1 *Skyraider* which first flew in May, 1945! Powered by a good old-fashioned reciprocating engine swinging a good old-fashioned prop, the A-1 goes on and on doing its job, defying replacement and teaching its pilots (many of whom were born after it was) what flying was all about in the old days. In continous production for more than ten years, more than 3,000 copies of 49 versions of seven basic types of *Skyraider* were built. The top two photos show A-1s of the Vietnamese Air Force (VNAF), the lower show an A-1H of VNAF 516 Squadron at Da Nang, loaded with fire bombs.
- *Via Geo. Letzter and Paul Stevens*

A-1E *Skyraider* in USAF markings as used by Air Commando units in COIN and rescue escort work.
- *Ira Ward*

Fusing 250-pound anti-personnel bombs slung beneath a VNAF A-1E.

USAF *Skyraiders* head for infiltration routes connecting Laos with Vietnam, these being frequent targets for Air Commando "Sandies." -*USAF*

Douglas AC-47 is of course the same DC-3/C-47 design that has served with distinction in peace and war for an almost unbelievable thirty-five years. In its newest role, the "Grand Old Lady" of aircraft mounts General Electric 7.62mm Miniguns, each capable of firing up to 6,000 rounds at ground targets requiring attention. The blaze of fire from the ship's side windows has earned the old type a new nickname, "Dragon ship."
- Ira Ward and USAF

Lockheed AC-130 *Hercules* gunship mounts four Miniguns and four M-61 Vulcan 20mm cannon, cameras and flares and high intensity lights for battlefield illumination. Photograph taken at Nha Trang Air Base. *- USAF*

Martin B-57E, American-built version of English Electric *Canberra*, paused at Alaskan air base in 1967 enroute to Vietnam. - *USAF*

B-57 in war paint heads for North Vietnamese target, April, 1966. - *USAF*

A 750-pound bomb falls away from a B-57 during strike at VC target. - *USAF*

Brand new Cessna A-37 with ferrying tanks installed ready for delivery to Vietnam. The popular light strike aircraft is now being supplied to the VANF. - *George Letzter*

The A-37's relatively slow speed allows it to bomb accurately and operate in weather unfavorable to high speed equipment. Its simplicity makes for easy maintenance.
- *George Letzter*

This 1967 shot shows A-37As armed with MK-82 and BLU-3/B napalm bombs in flight over South Vietnam.
- *USAF*

Seven-hundred-fifty pounders ready for delivery. The B-52's mission in Vietnam is one of the paradoxes of this strange war. The mighty earth-girdling strategic bomber has become our most feared *tactical* weapon! - USAF

Loading a B-52 at Guam. A typical mission sees 25 to 30 aircraft flying the 2,200 mile run to Vietnam, each loaded with fifty-one bombs (750 or 1,000 pound) carried internally and externally. - *USAF*

With a dozen non-nuclear high explosive bombs under each wing and 27 more tucked away inside, this B-52 was photographed leaving Guam. *USAF*

B-52D begins its 12-hour, 4500 mile trip from Guam to Vietnam and back.

Seconds from its target, giant B-52D *Stratofortress* opens its doors during 1967 raid. - *George Letzter*

A *Stratofortress* in action, as visualized by the author.

USAF Support Aircraft

Lockheed C-130 *Hercules* unloads supplies at Army Special Forces camp at Bu Dop, the short muddy strip being too short for landing. - *USAF*

Fairchild Hiller UC-123B *Provider* outfitted for "Ranch Hand" operations. - *George Letzter*

Ranch Hand C-123 spraying herbicides on jungle growths and thickets, wiping out possible Viet Cong ambush sites. The insignia of one Ranch Hand outfit includes the motto — "Only You Can Prevent Forests." - *USAF*

A *Provider* at work, as painted by the author.

A real workhorse of this war, the C-130 *Hercules.* Here a One-Thirty lands at dusk at Tay Ninh Air Base carrying troops and equipment.
- *USAF*

Kaman HH-43F *Huskie* settles into a clearing to pick up a wounded infantryman. The primary Air Force rescue aircraft in Vietnam, the *Huskie* has hung up an enviable record. - *Kaman*

Grumman HU-16 Search and Rescue aircraft made many successful rescues of pilots downed in the Gulf of Tonkin during early days of the war.
- *George Letzter*

Douglas EB-66, photographed here in Thailand, saw use as ECM platform and pathfinder for bombers.

Boeing KC-135 tanker may be termed military version of the 707/720 series of commercial airliners. This flying gas station has increased our bombers' range and loiter capability, greatly enhancing our striking power in the war.

McDonnell Douglas RF-101 *Voodoo* had to be withdrawn from tough recon assignments when enemy defenses were improved. - *USAF*

Sikorsky CH-3C lifts engineless Vietnamese H-34 from rice paddy where it crashed. - *USAF*

HH-3E in action, as seen in a painting by the author.

A reconnaissance version of the versatile *Phantom II,* the RF-4C has complex radar and photographic systems installed. - *Paul Stevens*

RF-4C on the prowl. This has become the mainstay of reconnaissance forces in the Vietnam War.
- *McDonnell Douglas*

Sikorsky HH-3E ''Jolly Green Giant'' at Danang Air Base. - *Paul Stevens*

Redoubtable old (first flight: 1947) Fairchild Hiller AC-119 *Packet* in flight near Nha Trang. It is popularly known as the "Flying Boxcar." - *USAF*

What the C-47 was to World War II, so is Lockheed's C-141 *Starlifter* to the air war in Vietnam. Most of the heavy freight crosses the Pacific in this enormous transport. - *USAF*

Lockheed C-140 *Jetstar* utility transport carries two crewmen and ten passengers on short hauls in the war zone. - *USAF*

More than 3,300 Cessna O-1 *Bird Dogs* have been built for military use. This is an O-1E from which an Air Force forward air controller (FAC) surveys a South Vietnam farm area. - *USAF*

The author's impression of combat flying in a lightplane.

Another businessman's plane gone to war is the Cessna O-2A, Air Force version of the popular *Super Skymaster*. Its duties include FAC missions, visual reconnaissance, target identification and marking, ground-air coordination and damage survey. Here, from top down, are the O-2A and O-2B. - *USAF*

North American Rockwell T-39 utility transport can carry from four to eight passengers. It is a military version of the *Sabreliner*. - *USAF*

USN/USMC Fighters

With afterburner ablaze and wingtips creating vortices in the catapult's steam, an F-8E *Crusader* of VF-211 is hurled from the deck of the *USS Bon Homme Richard* to perform its work over North Vietnam. - *USN*

F-4B *Phantoms* aboard the *USS Kitty Hawk.* - Lou Drendel

A brace of *Phantoms* from the *Kitty Hawk,* as painted by the author.

The fabulous *Phantom,* designed as fighter and attack bomber and since used for half a dozen other chores, seen here in USMC markings. Marine *Phantoms* have usually seen action in the ground attack role.
- George Letzter and Paul Stevens

F-4B *Phantom II* of Fighter Squadron 213 attached to the attack aircraft carrier *USS Kitty Hawk* (CVA-63) drops its ordnance on Viet Cong target. - *USN*

Landing Signal Officer eyes *Phantom* coming aboard the *USS Coral Sea* (CVA-43) after action in 1968.
- *USN*

The *USS Independence* (CVA-62) recovers a *Phantom* assigned to VF-84 - *McDonnell Douglas*

While operating from the *USS Hancock* this F-8E *Crusader* downed an enemy MIG. Note North Vietnamese flag beneath canopy. - *Paul Stevens*

Crusader is spotted on the Number 2 cat for launching aboard the *USS Bon Homme Richard* while operating on "Yankee Station" in the Gulf of Tonkin during 1967. - *USN*

Zuni rockets being loaded on a VF-51 *Crusader* on the deck of the *USS Ticonderoga*. The "Tico" was among the first carriers to launch raids against North Vietnam. *-USN*

No photo can show this view of a *Crusader's* launching as it is depicted by the author's art.

McDonnell Douglas A-4 *Skyhawk* is wheeled onto the starboard catapult of the
USS Oriskany before its mate has had time to retract its gear. - *USN*

A-1H *Skyraider* in experimental camouflage (later abandoned) aboard the *USS Kitty Hawk* in 1966. This aircraft was assigned to VA-115. - *George Letzter*

In this 1966 shot, a *Skyraider* was launched from the *USS Intrepid* (CVS-11). - *USN*

Author's painting shows typical A-1 *Skyraider* action.

45

Marine A-4C *Skyhawk* named "Topcat" as seen at Atsugi, Japan, Naval Air Station in May, 1967. This ship was 148472 assigned to VMA-311. - *George Letzter*

A-4 in VMA-121 markings leaves revetment for air strike. - *Paul Stevens*

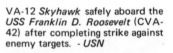

VA-12 *Skyhawk* safely aboard the *USS Franklin D. Roosevelt* (CVA-42) after completing strike against enemy targets. - *USN*

McDonnell Douglas KA-3B *Skywarrior* refuels *USS Kitty Hawk* - based *Skyhawks* which have just completed air strike in North Vietnam, 1968. - *USN*

Over the South China Sea, April 25, 1967. Lt. (jg) Alan R. Crebo of Greensburg, Ind., flies his badly damaged *Skyhawk* back to his carrier, the *USS Bon Homme Richard.* Crebo ejected alongside the carrier and was rescued by a destroyer. - *USN*

Latest version of the rugged and reliable *Skyhawk* series, this A-4F houses advanced avionics gear beneath bulge behind cockpit. - *Paul Stevens*

Working in the sound and fury of the *USS Ranger's* flight deck, catapult crewmen attach the bridle to a *Skywarrior* of VAH-2. - *USN*

KA-3B comes aboard the *Kitty Hawk*. The *Skywarrior* is the largest carrier-based aircraft in fleet service. The "Whale" is to the Navy what the KC-135 tanker is to the Air Force. - *Lou Drendel*

Lineup of combat weary A-3s from the *USS Constellation* on a California navy base. Originally a bomber, the A-3 has seen service as a tanker and ECM aircraft in Vietnam. - *Paul Stevens*

North American Rockwell RA-5C *Vigilante* is normally escorted to targets by fighters because of the limited visibility afforded its pilot. - *Paul Stevens*

Vigilante of RVAH-13 (*USS Kitty Hawk*) in short-lived experimental camouflage. - *George Letzter*

Six crewmen lift a 500-pound bomb to the multiple ejector racks of a VA-85 A-6A *Intruder* in this 1968 shot taken aboard the *USS America* (CVA-66). - *USN*

Mammoth size of the aircraft aboard modern carriers is apparent in this shot from the author's camera. Note six foot crewman walking around this Grumman VA-65 *Intruder*. - *Lou Drendel*

A-6A of VA-85 aboard the *USS Kitty Hawk* in 1966, with pair of *Phantoms* in background. - *George Letzter*

Thirty tons of bomber leaves the flight deck as this A-6A of VA-85 is launched. The *Intruder* carries a heavier and more varied load of ordnance than any other American naval attack airplane. - *Grumman*

Ling-Temco-Vought A-7A *Corsair II* of VA-147 is respotted after recovery aboard the *USS Ranger* in 1968. VA-147 was the first squadron to operate the new A-7 in combat. This particular ship was the first of its type to be lost in combat. - *USN*

A *Corsair II* picks up the wire aboard the *USS Ranger.* Designed for a high degree of survivability, the A-7 is equipped with considerable cockpit armor plating, self-sealing tanks and a dispersal of major components to minimize damage from hostile fire. - *USN*

USN/USMC Support Aircraft

Grumman's new C-2A *Greyhound* is designed to deliver cargo and personnel to carriers. Its duties are designated COD — carrier on-board delivery. - *Grumman*

Grumman E-2A *Hawkeye* ready for launch from the *USS Enterprise*. This early-warning aircraft's enormous radome develops enough lift in flight to offset its own weight.
- *Grumman*

LSO watches, and talks to, pilot of *Hawkeye* as he comes aboard the *Constellation* after a long patrol over the Gulf of Tonkin in 1966. - *USN*

Last of the Navy's flying boats, this Martin P-5 *Marlin* saw service in Operation "Market Time" patrolling coastal waters in search of Viet Cong supply barges. - *Lou Drendel*

Operating together in Operation "Market Time," this Lockheed P-2V *Neptune* and a Minesweeper combine forces to seek out enemy supply vessels. Below, Lockheed WV-1 *Super Constellation* early warning aircraft based at Danang.
- USN

North American Rockwell OV-10A *Bronco* is a light armed reconnaissance aircraft suited for counterinsurgency work. The first production aircraft flew in 1967. - *USN*

Sikorsky H-35 *Seahorse* landing on the amphibious assault ship *USS Okinawa* with mail picked up Danang. - *USN*

Kaman UH-2C *Seaprite,* a development of the original single-engine UH-2 series, is now aboard most carriers as the primary rescue aircraft. - *Kaman*   Below, Marines survey wreckage of 0-1 *Bird Dog* downed by ground fire at Vietnam Army outpost. - *USMC*

During a resupply mission, this Marine helicopter came under enemy fire, causing the intense activity shown here. Below, this 1963 picture shows Vietnamese Army troops leaving a Marine H-34 to launch an assault on enemy positions southwest of Danang. - *USMC*

U. S. Army

Huge Sikorsky H-37 *Mojave* demonstrates its lifting ability by hoisting an M-56 tank mounting a 106mm recoilless rifle. - *USA*

Grumman OV-1 *Mohawk* is a high performance observation aircraft. It has performed so successfully that the enemy has offered its troops rewards for shooting it down.
- *Richard C. Seeley*

Boeing-Vertol ACH-47 *Chinook* becomes a flying pillbox when equipped as this one is. Crew has dubbed it, "Easy Money," with the subtitle, "Guns-A-G0-G0".
- *J. Barnes*

Bell UH-1B *Iroquois* equipped with M-22 Armament system at An Khe, Vietnam, in early 1967 - *George Letzter*

Hughes OH-6 *Cayuse* light observation helicopter. This particular craft was shot down five times! Successful auto-rotations and the cannibalization of less-fortunate aircraft have kept it flying. Note minigun installation.
- *George Letzter*

Hiller H-23D *Raven* light observation helicopter.
- George Letzter

Bell AH-1G *Huey Cobra* attack helicopter is Army's primary close air support weapon. *- George Letzter*

A familiar sight at Tan Son Nhut Air Base at Saigon — a battered but still flying Boeing-Vertol CH-47 *Chinook*. *- Paul Stevens*

Sikorsky CH-54A *Skycrane* is employed in a variety of roles, from airlifting hospitals complete with operating rooms to dropping bombs. - *Sikorsky*

A *Chinook* airlifts a 105mm howitzer and assorted supplies to a new position. Such airlifting provides artillery with necessary mobility in this war that has no defined fronts. - *USA*

Bell UH-1D *Iroquois* here shows why it has been called the "jeep of the Vietnam War." - *Bell*

UH-1Bs depart, having off-loaded American infantrymen in contested area near Bien Hoa. - *Stars and Stripes*

To an injured walking soldier, nothing that flies is as beautiful as an Army medical evacuation chopper. - Bell

Chinook in one of its many roles, that of a bridge builder, here lowering a pontoon into position on a Vietnamese river. - USA

108946   63

About the author . . .

An artist who lives in Naperville, Ill., Lou Drendel's work has appeared in the Chicago *Sunday Tribune,* the *Journal* of the American Aviation Historical Society and his first book, "The Air War in Vietnam," which was an instant success. He is shown here suited out for a ride, courtesy of the Navy, in an F-4B *Phantom* — an experience he best describes in the painting above.